The Smart & Easy Guide To Forex Trading & Investing: The Ultimate Foreign Exchange Strategy, Currency Markets, Forecasting Analysis, Risk Management Handbook and Primer

Richard Norris

Legal Stuff

COPYRIGHT

Copyright © 2013 Checkmate Marketing Group LLC. All rights reserved worldwide.

No part of this publication may be replicated, redistributed, or given away in any form without the prior written consent of the author and publisher.

Checkmate Marketing Group LLC

LIMITATION OF LIABILITY

THE MATERIALS IN THIS BOOK ARE PROVIDED "AS IS" WITHOUT ANY EXPRESS OR IMPLIED WARRANTY OF ANY KIND INCLUDING WARRANTIES OF MERCHANTABILITY, NONINFRINGEMENT OF INTELLECTUAL PROPERTY, OR FITNESS FOR ANY PARTICULAR PURPOSE. IN NO EVENT SHALL OR ITS AGENTS OR OFFICERS BE LIABLE FOR ANY DAMAGES WHATSOEVER (INCLUDING, WITHOUT LIMITATION, DAMAGES FOR LOSS OF PROFITS, BUSINESS INTERRUPTION, LOSS OF INFORMATION, INJURY OR DEATH) ARISING OUT OF THE USE OF OR INABILITY TO USE THE MATERIALS, EVEN IF HAS BEEN ADVISED OF THE POSSIBILITY OF SUCH LOSS OR DAMAGES.

The prices on the market are relatively easy to predict, since these usually follow a certain pattern. Plus, there are fees for exchanging or commissions charged when trading online, allowing you to keep more of your profit. There are fees associated with brokers, but the fee is relatively small when compared to other investment markets.

If you are serious about getting into the forex market, the following terminology can get you started on the right path:

- Spot Market: This is the time frame, usually one day, for buying and selling currencies.

- Exchange Rate: The value of the currency that is exchanged for another currency.

- Currency Pair: This refers to the two currencies that always make up a trade. One is sold, while the other is purchased.

- Base Currency: This is the first currency featured in a currency pair.

- Counter Currency: The second currency featured in a currency pair.

- Broker: This is going to be the person who can match a seller and buyer together, though they do charge a fee for this.

- Sell Quote: This is a quote of what the base currency can be sold for. This is also called the bid price.

- Buy Quote: This is the price in which you can buy the base currency for.

Top Currencies in the Forex Market

There are several aspects that affect the price of currency, such as the economy and politics within a country. Other factors include inflation and current interest rates. A country can try to control the value of their currency through lowering the value or by raising the price through buying their own currency on a large scale, however, this is referred to as flooding the market. Due to the sheer size of the forex market, it is almost impossible for any country to have control over the value of their currency for a long period of time. Due to this, many investors look at the forex market as one of the most fair investment opportunities out there.

Every currency in the world of the forex market is given a three-letter code that is used for investors to know just which currency is which. The most common that are seen are USD (US dollars), JPY (Japanese yen), EUR (European euros), GBP (United Kingdom pounds), CHF (Swiss francs), and AUD (Australian dollars). These are the top currencies that investors are looking for, and they have been considered at the top for several years on the forex market.

When looking at the prices that are found in the forex market, they always appear in pairs. The first set of currencies is referred to as the base, which is always held at one, the second currency is the quote. The quote is meant to show how much it costs to buy one unit of the base currency. For example:

USD/EUR = 0.8419

EUR/USD = 1.1882

The base currency is strong when the quote currency increases. When the quote currency begins to decrease, the value of the base currency will weaken. When looking at these quotes, it is important to note that these are quotes that are considered to be at an 'ask' or 'bid' price. The ask price refers to what the seller will sell the currency for, while also buying the quoted currency. The bid price refers to what the buyer will pay for the base currency while selling the currency being quoted. For example:

USD/CAD 1.2392 1.2397

This example shows that with 1.2397 Canadian dollars, you can purchase one US dollar. It also shows that you can sell one US dollar for 1.2392 Canadian dollars. For those who are having trouble with this concept, there are tons of currency calculators online that a person can use in order to figure out just how much something would be.

There are any new currencies that are emerging into the market, and these are currencies that a person needs to watch out for, as they could become more dominant. These are:

- CNY (China yuan)

- HKD (Hong Kong dollar)

- CZK (Czech koruna)

- HUF (Hungarian Forint)

- KRW (Korean Won)

- PLN (Polish Zloty)

- INR (Indian Rupee)

- MXN (Mexican Peso)

- ZAR (South African Rand)

- SGD (Singapore dollar)

- THB (Thai Baht)

These currencies are currently limited to whom they can trade with. For example, the yuan can only be traded by financial institutions and onshore companies. For those who are interested the USD/CNY rate is at 8.2770. The Chinese government has been asked to reevaluate the value of their currency, yet they have not complied. The reason for this is that the higher the value their currency, the stronger their banking system is getting, along with strengthening their economy.

Another example is the koruna, this is a free floating currency that has been around since 1997. Foreign investors have access to the local market, and many London banks are active in this currency. The interest rate of this currency is driven by offshore banks.

The Euros Performance in the Forex Market

The Forex is the largest trading market in the world, and is often called the foreign exchange market. The Forex does not have a closing time or a trading place, instead, there is over $2 trillion traded each day, all day long, during business days of each week. On the Forex, a person will find six currency pairs that dominate the market. These are:

- Euro and US Dollar

- Japanese yen and US Dollar

- US dollar and the Swiss Franc

- The Australian dollar and US dollar

- British pound and US dollar

- US dollar and Canadian dollar

On the Forex Market, these currencies are going to operate differently, as well as fluctuate each day. With the market, the Euro holds a vital role. This is because the Euro represent twelve countries within Europe. These countries are in the European Union and are Austria, Belgium, Finland, France, Germany, Greece, Ireland, Italy, Luxembourg, Netherlands, Portugal, Spain and Sweden. There are only two of the European Union, Denmark and the UK that do not have the euro as their official currency. Before these countries accepted the euro as their main currency, the system had their current currency locked into be the equivalent in value to the euro. Due to the countries coming together, this helped to increase the value of the euro. When compared to the US dollar, the euro is worth about 90 cents of each US dollar.

When looking at the Forex market, the use of a single currency for many countries has its advantages, but also has a few disadvantages. The biggest benefit of the euro is the fact that the exchange rate is lowered, making it easier for investments from around the globe. Most of countries are a bit hesitant to import or export in currency other than what they utilize since it could result in a huge loss of profit, and since the euro is established for many countries, this eliminates this risk. There is also the benefit of eliminating conversion fees which can add up over time, despite the fact that the initial fee is rather small.

A person also needs to note that with just one form of currency for several countries, the market becomes deeper, making the market much more liquid than it was a few years ago. The reason that the market becomes deeper has to deal with how consumers are going to spend money. Since the euro spans across several countries, statistics suggest that this will increase the spending on the stock market that people do.

Usually, the Forex market is dominated by the US dollar. However, with the euro taking over, it looks as though the euro is becoming one of the more dominant forms of currency in the Forex market. Through the euro becoming more dominant, it leads people able to use this all over the world, without having to exchange their currency.

Japanese Yen vs. US Dollar in the Forex Market

The official currency in Japan is the Japanese Yen. It is the third most traded form of currency on the Forex market. When looking at all the currencies on the Forex market, people will find that the yen and the US dollar are very compatible. In order to understand how the market works, it is vital that a person have an understanding of currency.

The Yen was first recognized in 1870 as a form of currency and was modeled after the financial system in Europe. The yen lost most of its value after WWII, yet it has consistently risen order to be more comparable to the US dollar today. The value of the yen is going to be determined by the Forex market and this is through the supply and demand principle. When the demand for the yen is high, such as when people are looking to exchange their current currency for the yen, the value of the yen is going to increase. Likewise, when there is little trading for the yen, then the value is going to decrease. It wasn't until 1971 that the yen was starting to gain momentum thanks to the failure of the Bretton Woods System. Up until this time, most people would state that the yen was seldom thought of, even though it was a noticeable type of currency that should have gained more attention.

The Japanese government has long been worried that if the value of the yen increased that the export business would decrease. This is because it would increase the cost of products that are made in Japan and ultimately affect how other countries were purchasing products. Due to this, the government often intervened in the Forex market in order to change the value of the yen, even though this did little to nothing as the value of the yen kept to steadily climb. The yen did decrease as the price of oil increased from 1974 to 1976. During the late 70's and 80's, the yen fluctuated in value. The yen began to surpass the US dollar in the late 80's thanks to the trading system being in full swing.

When more countries began to invest in Japan, while many companies started to move to Japan to have their products manufactured here, the value of the yen increased dramatically. Due to the higher value of the yen, Japanese companies began to look for cheaper and more effective ways of producing products in order to offset the cost of exporting and importing goods.

There has always been many traders who are exchanging the yen for the US dollar. Due to this, the exchange rates offered through the Forex market are very important. The rate of exchange is going to have a direct effect on the price of products and services, as well as whether a country will have goods exported. There are those who can predict the rate over time, after they have looked at the government policies in effect for a country, the current events happening around the globe, as well as supply and demand. The Forex does have flexible rates, which means some days are better than other.

For those who are serious about getting into the Forex market, they should remember that it takes a professional to know what should and should not be done. There are several people who spend their whole life chasing the perfect trade and the way in which a person should trade to ensure perfection. Those who are looking at the yen and the US dollar will find that the value of these are more comparable now than they have ever been. Due to this, it is one of the major currencies that traders are working with.

Exotic Currencies: Their Definition and Impact on Forex Market

When dealing with exotic currency's, many people are unaware of what this really is. This is currency that is defined as having little liquidity and can only be dealt with in a limited capacity. It is not a currency that is considered a major or a minor currency. A few examples of these currencies are the Australian dollar, the New Zealand dollar and the Canadian dollar. Major currencies are the Euro, Japanese yen, the Swiss franc, the British pound and the German mark. It is important to note that the exotic currency is just as important as the major currencies on the market.

The Forex market plays a huge role with financial institutions, as most of these bands and reserves utilize the market in order to make profit. These profits are offered to all those who are interested in buying into the market. The entire world is becoming more dependent on one another thanks to the state of trade and foreign investments. Any country that is having a hard economical time will find this can affect their interest rate on their currency, which can affect their performance on the Forex market. In conjunction, the health of the economy for most countries is going to depend on the value of their currency and whether this is increasing or decreasing.

When it comes to the banks that use the Forex market, many of these banks will find that they make anywhere from forty to sixty percent of their profit from trading currencies, and this is only when they invest around twenty to thirty percent of their funds into the market. Most Americans have not been aware of the Forex market, as it has only recently became a commodity for the public to trade into. Plus, the minimum account the person would need to have has been beyond the means of most average citizens. It was once that a person had to have a minimum of $200,000 in their account to trade, this has been lowered to $10,000.

It important to remember that the foreign exchange market is dominated by:

- The US Dollar (USD)

- The British pound(GBP)

- Japanese yen (JPY)

- European euro (EUR)

- Swiss franc (CHF)

These five currencies account for seventy percent of the trades that occur in North America. The exotic currencies that account for three to seven percent of the total market are:

- New Zealand dollar (NZD)

- Australian dollar (AUD)

- Canadian dollar (CAD)

- French franc (XPF)

When the exotic and the major currencies are combined, this makes up the list of all the currencies that are being traded on the Forex market.

The top three traded currencies are the US dollar, the European euro, and the Japanese yen. The US dollar (USD) is given its strength the the Index. The Index is a basic measurement tool that is used to determine whether the value of the dollar is strong, as is the case when the index number is high, or if the value is weak, as is the case when the index number is low. The dollar has become a bit weaker over the past two decade due to the world's views on the financial policies, namely the budget deficits in the US.

The Euro is the currency of eleven nations, including Spain, France, Italy, Belgium, Austria, Portugal, Luxembourg, Finland, Germany, the Netherlands and Ireland. These eleven nations account for almost twenty percent of the economy in the world. The European Union is considered to be the US's largest foreign market that they deal with, with trading between the two having been occurring for over two decades.

The Japanese yen continues to dominate the market, and is still seen as a global power in the market place. The yen has become the third most traded currency in all of the world. This is in thanks to the Japanese government giving the time and knowledge to making their economy the shape that it is in.

Foreign Exchange Markets Overview and What the Crossing Currency in the Forex Market means to Traders

The barter system was the method that most countries used when they were first getting established. If one country was in need of cattle, while the other country needed lumber, they would simply trade one product for the other. This type of trading was great for several years, though it now has many limitations to it. The benefits that nations saw when this was in play was that it could be great to have a system of exchange for a country. Each country had something to trade, and the most sought after items were gold and silver.

Gold and silver coins were used most often and this is where the pound sterling, the name of the British currency was found. There was paper money during this time, and it quickly became the choice to go to instead of carrying around gold. This is why many banks started to put their gold somewhere else, as there were not many people who were exchanging paper money for gold. This is why many banks put their gold reserves into Fort Knox, and then inflation set into the country.

The Bretton conference at the end of the WWII, had nations reach a currency system agreement that was based on the US dollar which resulted in a fixed exchange rate. With this in place, the dollar was based in value off of gold, while other currencies put their value to the dollar. After this was in place, fluctuation started which has the value of the currency increasing and decreasing sporadically.

The Forex market allows traders to take advantage of this fluctuation. The old saying of buy low and sell high is what most traders are aiming for. This is especially true if the person believes the euro is going to increase in value when compared to other currency. Margin trading is in place when traders work with the Forex market. With this type of trading a person does not have to have the money they are trading, they simply have to have one percent of the money they are trading. For example, as long as the person has $10,000, they can trade up to $100,000. This is great for those who may be looking for trades that is going to allow them to get this done quickly, while making an attractive return. However, with this being said, there are some risks the person needs to be aware of.

When it comes to risks, the person will find that many aggressive traders find that they can lose and profit with a 30% fluctuation each day. With this being said, a trader has to know the market in order to ensure they are not losing each day, yet loses are pretty much inevitable. Due to the fact that there are no limits or restrictions on trading, a person can make this up if they have the know how.

Though most people focus on the individual trader, when it comes to the Forex market that are many commercial traders that are involved. In the Forex market, the banks and financial institutions are some of the biggest traders. There are many complaints out there related to banks and hedge funds being involved in the trading, stating that these types of traders have too much interest in what is being traded. Change of manipulation does exist when the largest amounts of currency is owned by financial institutions. No matter what a persons stance is on this topic, they will find that the Forex market is still a great way to make money.

Forex Traders and Crossing Currency

There is excitement and profit to be had when trading on the Forex market. However, for those who are wanting to succeed, they must understand the terms and the rules for trading on the market. Those who are interested in learning from someone will find that banks and brokers are often the best source of information.

Exchanging currency refers to when a person wants to trade one type of currency for another. This is often referred to as crossing currency. This is the main goal of those who are trading on the Forex market. For example, when a company wants their US dollars changed to Japanese yen, a broker is the one to do this for them. There are several people who trade currency in order to make a profit off of the trade. This happens when a currency is purchased low and then sold once the currency increases in value.

Those who are serious about earning money on the Forex market will find that crossing currency is the best way to do this. There is over two trillion dollars that is exchanged on the market each day and it makes it simple for every trader to get in on the trading happening. The US dollar, Japanese yen and the Euro are the top three currencies that are traded, and they are most often traded into other forms of currency.

The process of crossing currency can be very hard for people to understand. The biggest benefit to using this method is knowing how the market works and how trading is completed. Crossing currency does allow a person to make a large profit without losing much if any capital. Those who invest $500, with an ideal market could earn over $100,000. The flexibility that is allowed for the trader and investor is another reason why the market is one in which many traders are interested in. The quickness of the trade ensures that the person is never stuck with currency that they cannot sell. In addition, those who use a pre-set platform can always back out of deal if the pre-requisites for the deal are not being met.

The ability to profit in markets that are rising and falling is one of the reasons so many people flock to the Forex market. With a stock market, the only way a person can make money is if the market is on the rise, these investors lose money when there is a bear market. However, with the Forex, this is not the case. Even when currency is down, an investor can stand to make quite a bit of money. In addition, the Forex market is always open, which gives investors greater reign of freedom when it comes to making their investments. Thanks to the Internet, a person can trade at all times of the day, every day of the week.

There are several methods that you can use in order to learn about trading with the Forex market. For those who are looking online, they can find free demos, and many website that are going to offer free and valuable information on how this process can be done. For those who are just starting a mini Forex account can be the best way to learn new methods while getting a better comprehension of the market.

Investment Myths Associated with the Forex Market

There are several misconceptions or myths that new traders buy into once they start trading on the market. Most people see trading taking place and think that anyone can do it, however, that is not the case. It does take a lot of knowledge about the market and strategy in order to earn profit from trading currency. For those who are new to the market, they need to ensure that they are not getting caught up in the myths that are out there, as this can ruin their chances of becoming successful with trading since it distorts the reality of this type of work. The following information should help you to ensure you keep your reality check when dealing with the Forex Market.

- Protect your Investments

You are going to find that most people think that as long as your investments are still locked into the market that they are safe, however, this is not the case. Even when you have investments that you are going to trade later, you must actively protect these. In order to do this you have to be on your toes and know what the market is doing each and every minutes of the day. Due to the length of time that the Forex market is open, there are several things that can wrong very fast.

Using the Forex market is a not a way in which a person can get rich quick. This does require that the person put through and research into each and every decision they are making. Yet, the person also needs to keep in mind that they have to take some risk in order to see the big profits. Those who take a large risk will find that they could get a large profit, however, the person still needs to be prepared for the worst that can happen. The good thing is that the more you prepare, the better off you are going to be.

Those who are new to this and want to ensure that they are doing all that they can do in order to make profits will find taking a class or two on the Forex can be helpful. In addition, talking to someone who does this can also prove to be very beneficial. You will need to know that even if you take classes, do your research and the like, there are going to be times in which you lose money. Even the most seasoned of professionals can lose money when it comes to the Forex market.

- Leverage

Leverage refers to what a person can use in order to make more money, even if they do not have that much to start out with. This is something that can be great for traders, but it can also prove to be the downfall of traders who are not careful in what they are doing. Those who use leverage as it should be used will find that they can make money in shorts amounts of time. However, this is not as easy to do as most people seem to think it is.

Those who are able to use leverage in order to gain more money are usually those who have been in the trading business for several years. Thus, these people have a wealth of knowledge and expertise when it comes to trading. This is what a person needs in order to use leverage as a way to make money, rather than lose it.

Due to the way that the Forex market is working, most everyone can trade for quite a bit more than what they really have in their portfolio. However, those who do this are often not aware that they are taking a huge risk. Just because you can trade above your portfolio, does not mean that you should do this. Those who know how to leverage will find this easier, but a newbie to the market needs to take their time and learn the process, because the person does not know when they should stop. You have to have some trades under your belt before you start this type of behavior.

Those who enter into the Forex market and hear tons of myths that are being told as facts should be certain that they know the truth. You need to protect your investments actively, rather than thinking they are safe just sitting on the market. In addition, you need to understand what leverage is and how to use this before you jump into this technique. You are not going to get rich in a hurry with the Forex market. Those who say they get rich quick are usually those traders who have been doing this for years and have advanced knowledge o the market and currency. When dealing with the Forex market, it is imperative that you do your research and think before you act.

The Exchange Rate and Its Impact on the Forex Market

For those who are just beginning in the trading world, it can be daunting to hear information about the exchange rate. Words like euros, yen, francs, dollars, points, floating rates and the like are thrown about and it can be devastating to someone who has never heard these terms. However, you must know how exchange rates work in order to truly understand how to work with the Forex market. Those who have no idea about the exchange rate will find that it does not take them long to make a bad trade that results in money that is lost. The exchange rate is a huge concept to understand, yet it does affect the way in which currency is traded.

The exchange rate is basically referring to how one currency is valued when compared to another currency. For example, if you were to exchange a dollar to dimes, you would know the exchange rate would mean ten dimes for every dollar. In this type of equation the exchange rate would have a formula of DOL/DIM=.10. And the exchange rate for this scenario is going to go either way, for ten dimes, you could exchange for one dollar.

When you are dealing with the forex market, the definition for the exchange rate simply swaps out the currency to include foreign currencies. For example, you would be dealing with yens, pounds, euros and the like. In this example, you are looking at trading euros for US dollars, it would be expressed as EUR/USD = 1.1023. This means that every euro is worth around 1.1023 US dollars. In reverse, it would be USD/EUR = .9071, meaning that if you were interested in obtaining 1000 euros, you would pay around $1,102.30 US dollars.

The exchange rate does fluctuate and can move up or down, which is really where people start to become confused. It is best to use an example that is closer to home in order to understand this concept. With the above example of dollars and dimes, let's say that a store only wants customers to pay in dimes. If you go in to buy a gallon of water which costs $1.50, you would have to have $2 to turn into dimes, and simply buy the water. However, the problem arises when people start to run out of dimes, there is a demand of the currency thus people start to make deals. For example, you need the $1.50 water in dimes, so you give someone the $2 and tell them to simply give you the fifteen dimes you need. With this type of example, the exchange rate has been changed because the value of the dime has increased. This means that every dollar is worth more dimes than it was before.

Using this same basic principle when applying to the currency market is simple. If you were to buy goods from the Japanese market, you are expected to use yens in order to purchase these. The US dollars you have will have to be exchanged for yens in order to make the deal work. If there are people rushing to buy products from Japan, who are having to exchange their US dollars, francs or the like, then the value of the yen is going to increase. Meaning that you are going to spend more money for the product or service you are purchasing.

When an economy is strong, those who watch for these periods know that they can make more money if they invest into products or businesses that are in the country. It is going to involve exchanging their currency for the currency that the country accepts. This is supply and demand at its best.

Along with supply and demand, there are other factors that will affect the exchange rate a person is seeing. For one, the interest rate is a huge player in the exchange rate. For example, you will earn an interest rate on any currency that you have, the higher the interest rate the more money you have. Thus, when a currency starts earning a higher interest rate, people flock to exchanging their current currency for the higher earning currency. This is going to make the exchange rate increase, since there are so many people that are trying to do this.

The inflation rate also plays a major role in the exchange rate. The higher the inflation rate, the lower value of the currency. Likewise, the lower the inflation rate, the higher the value of the currency. Thus, when inflation hits, most currency is exchanged for other currency in countries in which inflation is not as high.

Trading with other countries is also a huge contributing factor to the exchange rate. The higher the economy, the more valuable their currency becomes. For countries that do a lot of exporting, they have a higher economy since they are making sales to other countries. For example, the US buys oil from Canada, meaning that the Canadian dollar is higher in value than the US dollar because the economy is in better shape.

There are tons of other aspects that affect the currency exchange rate, yet this does give you a basic understanding of how things could go in the market. It is important that you monitor these trends as this can dictate what type of move you need to make on the market.

The Forex Market and Global Expansion

In 1973, the foreign market was developed, it was a few decades later that the forex market started. Though this is the time frame for the forex market, there has always been trading of currency in the market. The first currency exchange can be traced back to the Middle East when coins from one country was exchanged for coins from other countries. Transactions became easier once paper money was introduced to the market. The forex market has encouraged strong trading among the countries, and brings many benefits to all those countries who do participate in the market.

When the Forex market was established there were several modifications that had to be made to the market, these include:

- The Bretton Woods Accord that was established in 1994, which organized a new world wide economical order. It was initiated by the US, Great Britain and France. This was when the US dollar (USD) become the standard form of currency in which determined the value of other currencies.

- In December of 1971, the Smithsonian Agreement replaced the Bretton Woods Accord. Most aspects remained the same, yet it allowed for more fluctuation on the foreign exchange market.

- The free floating system replaced the Smithsonian Agreement in 1978. This allowed no limitations to be placed on investors and traders, leaving it open for all those who wanted to get in on the market. It also allowed for currency to go whichever way it would naturally go without any interference from countries. Currently, currency fluctuates in value about every 4.8 seconds.

The forex market encompasses the entire world, and it is one of the biggest indicators of growth throughout the nations. The size of the market is hard to visualize as it is never ending. One transaction always leads to more following transactions, which does make it hard for a person to grasp just how big this market is. Most of the current trades occur in New York, London and Japan. The only time in which the market is stopped is on Friday, since Japan closes business and it also is a one day window before Europe starts to open their business. The majority of traders that participate in the market are from banks, brokerages and investment companies.

The Oil Marketplace and Its Affect on the Forex Market

There are several people who question why they should care what the price of oil is unless they are involved in the selling or buying of oil? This is a question that has merits, yet, with trading currencies, this is something that a person needs be aware of. The price of oil affects the way in which currency prices increase or decrease. For decades, the economy can be determined by the price of oil. When it comes to oil and the economy of a country, a few simple facts must be remembered:

1. Those countries that have supplies of oil are going to be more rich in terms of their economy when the price of oil is high.

2. Those countries that do not have oil are going to be most beneficial when the price of oil is low, while their economy is going to suffer when prices of oil increase.

3. The economy directly correlates to the value of the currency. When the economy is good, the value of their currency is higher.

4. When the economy goes down, the value of currency also declines.

The oil prices of 2005, which fluctuated consistently is one of the best ways to show how the price of oil will affect the economy. Basic economical principles state that when the price of oil is high, consumers are not going to spend as much. This is because the consumer may have to offset other costs in order to afford oil. This is going to remain a constant as long as countries are dependent upon oil that is petroleum based. All goods are priced according to the price of oil. For example, product and supply costs are going to increase when the price of oil is higher. The spending for consumers increases when oil prices are higher in order to heat their home and fuel their automobile. All of this combines to send the economy in a downward spiral that is going to continue until the economy hits a certain point, and the economy starts to shift up again.

There are several experts who always make predictions on just what the price cap for oil will be. A few years ago, experts said that oil would never go over $40 a barrel, yet that summer saw a barrel going for a little over $40. There are several aspects that can affect the price of oil including the weather in the country producing this oil, politics and the supply and demand. A barrel of oil has hit $70 in the past few years, which is much more than any expert had ever predicted. Conservatives now believe that $80 a barrel is the price that most countries will pay, while others state that this could be well over $100 a barrel.

The exchange rate of currency is often correlated with the health of the economy within a country. When an economy is at its best, the exchange rate is a higher value. When the economy is faltering, the exchange rate is lower. With this in mind, the following facts make much more sense to traders:

1. Countries that produce and export oil will have currency which rises in value.

2. Countries that import oil will have currency with a low value.

3. Trades that are the most profitable are going to be those countries that export oil and those countries that import oil.

With this being known, experts are always interested in trades between Canada and China. This is because Canada produces a significant amount of oil and is considered the 9th largest exporter in oil. The Chinese market has been paying attention to Canada because Canada proves for the US, which China will match in terms of need for oil. This scenario means that the Canadian dollar is one of the most interesting trades that a person could make.

Japan imports almost all of its oil, with only having 1% on hand for their own use. When the price of oil rises, the Japanese economy starts to slump as they are spending more to import their oil into the country. The value of the yen drops when this occurs.

History has shown us that the price of oil cannot continue to rise without hitting a breaking point. Consumers will start to cut their demand for oil and gas, which is going to help the price of oil stabilize. Until then though, the fluctuation of currency value will continue to happen.

Elliot Wave Theory for the Forex Market

The Elliot Wave Theory is one of the least understood theories associated with trading on the Forex market, yet is also the best known. This was developed in the 1920's by Ralph Nelson Elliot and was basically used as a way to calculate trends on the stock market. However, the mathematical theory that it utilizes can also be used to predict behavior with crowds. The basic principle of the theory is that the market will move in a series of five swings up and three swings down, and this is repeated. However, anyone who has studied this theory knows that it is not this simple, as there is more to it than simply finding the grove of the swings.

This theory is all about timing, and this is what makes it harder to understand for many people. There is no time limit on when the swings are going to occur, which makes it hard to figure out just what type of swing the market is in at the moment. In all reality, mathematics has shown that within a swing there are smaller swings that a person has to calculate for. Due to the complexity of calculating when the swings are going to be, many people state that if twenty experts on the Elliot Wave theory were in the same room, not one of these experts would reach an agreement on which way the market is heading.

There are two basic principles that a person must remember when they are dealing with the Elliot Wave Theory.

- For every action there is a reaction that follows.

If the action of currency is that the currency drops, then the reaction is that people are going to buy. When people buy the currency, the demand is going to increase while supply decreases, making the price of the currency go back up. The key to figuring out when to buy is knowing when the trade is going to be profitable for the trader.

- There are 5 waves within the main trend that is going to be followed by three more waves that are meant to correct the trend, these are referred to as the 5-3 move. The 5-3 waves is meant to get currency back to where it started, and complete the cycle. This is where the majority of people have a hard time understanding this theory. The 5-3 wave is almost like a never ending ripple within a pond, there are more 5-3 waves within the wave, that makes it harder to figure out just where the larger wave starts and the subset waves begin. A few things to remember about the 5-3 wave is:

1. The 5 waves are labeled as 1, 2, 3, 4, and 5 and are often referred to as impulses

2. The 3 minor waves are called corrections and are referred to as a, b, and c.

3. Each of the correction waves consist of another 5-3 series waves.

4. The main 5-3 wave remains a constant, yet the time frame of the waves is going to be different each time this occurs. The time frame can be going on for decades, or just minutes.

Those who have had success with this theory state that understanding and benefiting from this theory is all about the timing. The key for most traders is finding when wave 3 hits and making their move. This is the wave that most traders finds minimizes their risk while increasing their profit.

There is a ton of interpretation that can be used with this theory and this is why there are so many people who do not succeed with this method. You have to identify the patterns and then see if these patterns are going to hold for a set period of time, during which you have to make the decision to sell or buy.

The Bollinger Band Technical Indicator

The Bollinger Band technical indicator is employed by professionals to help compare the relative price and the volatility of a currency or product over a specific time period. It was created by John Bollinger. The indicator is comprised of three bands, the moving average, the upper band and the lower band. The upper band is the average plus two standard deviators, while the lower band is the average minus the two standard deviations. The idea around the indicator is that it is meant to show the price action of a currency.

It is hard for someone who wants to get involved with the market to simply start using this indicator. There are professionals who constantly take new courses on this indicator in order to get a better grasp on what it offers. With this being said, if you are interested in it, it is suggested that you look at your local college and see if there are any investing classes that will be offering this information. The more you understand the indicator, the more likely you are going to succeed with using it. There are those who can pick this up with little to no instruction, while others struggle with the indicator. With this being said there are a few rules that you can use in order to grasp the subject a bit better.

1. The Bolinger bands are only meant to provide a relative definition of price. This is not an exact science as there are many aspects that can throw off these calculations. Through the findings with the indicator it can better help you to make a decision as to whether to buy or sell.

2. You should never take the indicators you use and relate this to one another. Among the indicators, you can use momentum, open interest, market data and volume. The rule of thumb with this is that you cannot use two indicators that deal with volume since the results would not be correct.

3. You can see price patterns with these bands when they are used correctly. You will not see an exact price, but you will see the highs and lows, as well as the shifts in price. With this information it can help you to make a decision as to whether the currency is worth holding onto or selling at the moment.

4. The average price of a currency is not going to be as exact as the person would think. There are defaults associated with this indicator that means the price that is average may not be a price that has been present on the market. This is not good for those who are considering crossovers.

Those who decide to use the indicator should realize that this is for informational purposes only. This is not meant to be a way to signal whether you should sell or buy at that moment. This is strictly meant to help your investment decision. Though many professionals use this, they also state that they rely on their own experience and the feeling they have about an investment. This is just to assist you in proving that the gut feeling you have is worth looking into.

Fibonacci and the Forex Market

The idea of the forex market is to make money and those who follow the Fibonacci strategy within this market will find that this is what this strategy is about. The idea around this strategy is that it allows significant returns on what is traded. This works in conjunction with the Elliot Wave theory that was discussed earlier. The idea is to identify the points in a market that are going to make the person the biggest return on their investment, which is exactly what the Elliot Wave theory is all about.

Leonardo Pisano was called Fibonacci from 1170 to 1250. He was a mathematician that was simply brilliant, and there is a whole spectrum of math that is named after him, and even has a scholarly journal that has his name as the title. He is responsible for the introduction of the modern decimal system, as well as many number theories. His mathematical theories were reverend by many and he became fairly popular among the elite in society.

Those who trade on the Forex market have many thanks to give to Fibonacci as it was his ideas that have been expanded upon that allows traders to start seeing connections in the market.

Forex Trading Economical Indicators

When looking at the Forex market, there are many aspects and factors that can affect how currency is traded. Those who are just starting out will find that having the knowledge of what makes the forex market work is going to help them with their trades. Knowing how the market can fluctuate from day to day, even hour to hour is going to allow the person to significantly reduce their chances of losses. For the most part, the changes in the forex market are economical in nature, as a person will find that any shift in a countries economy can cause a shift in the value of the currency.

Within each country, there are several factors that affect just how strong or weak the economy is. For example, the current government policies and current events within the country can make or break an economy. For example, if a country were to be suffering from a war, then the economy is going to be hard, meaning the currency value could be relatively low. It is important that a person read the reports on the economies that are comprised from professionals before they make any decision as to what they should do with their currency. A broker can be the best source of information when looking at what to do with the currency. These reports are released daily and they are going to be the one way in which a trader can spot the trends of what may happen with the market.

When it comes to analyzing the forex market, the current events and the state of the economy in the country is the top piece of information that is used. Unemployment, the state of the government, housing statistics and the like can all make the forex market change. For example, when a country is in a good state when it comes to the current affairs happening, the forex market is going to reflect this good condition. When there are large numbers of people who are unemployed, the inflation rate rises and the housing market falls, then the currency is going to decrease in value. There are those who tend to overlook these facts in hopes that they will not affect the market, yet those who do this are taking a huge risk.

The GDP, also knowns as the gross domestic product, is also used to look at the market to see of any changes that could be coming to the currency. This figure is basically the market value of all the goods and services that are produced within the country in question. This is usually measured in a year time frame, rather than just months or weeks. Through using a larger time frame, the statistics are more reliable. Yet, this figure cannot be used alone when wanting to determine where the market is going. In addition, this measurement is usually already calculated after the economy of a country has started to show signs of distress or improvement.

The retail sales report is the third factor that is used to analyze the market. This is the total of all the retail stores within a country, though not every retail store is included. This is more of a rough estimate of how much the retail sales have amounted to. This points to whether the economy is slumping or fairing well, as consumers tend to buy more in a time of a good economy and bad less when the economy is fading.

The industrial production report shows the production in industries throughout an economy and can indicate just what state the economy is rather easily. When the industries produce more, it means that consumers are using more products, the country is exporting more, and basically shows a healthy economy. When this occurs, most traders see this as a good time to trade since it shows the economy is working as it should.

The consumer price index, or CPI, is the last factor that is used when analyzing the market. This index measures the changes in consumer prices in around two hundred different categories. This allows traders to see whether a country is making money with what they are producing, or if they are losing money. This in turn, reflects whether the economy is doing good or bad.

It is important to note that many of these factors can be used alone in determining whether the market is a good or bad time for trading. Yet, most of these factors need to be used in conjunction with other factors in order to get a clearer picture of what to do.

Forex Software: Tips for Choosing the Right One

There are many software programs on the market that are designed to help a person get started in the Forex market. These are both desktop and web based, meaning that you do have a choice in choosing which is best suited for your needs. Many brokers offer software packages to their clients in order to help them in the forex market, to specifically gain a better understanding of what the forex market is and how this works. Keep in mind that many web based platforms have a free demo you can try out, which is always good as this can give you a good idea of what you are going to need.

When it comes to choosing the software, the first decision is what type of to use. The web based and desktop version can offer the same type of information, thus there is no need to worry that once is more complete than the other. However, you will want to read reviews on what is offered and whether this is helpful.

Secondly, consider your Internet connection. This software will need to be updated in order to stay current with the trends in the forex market. Thus, dial up is more than likely not the best choice. DSL or broadband Internet is the best option for running this software since it is faster.

Also consider the security that the software is offering. Web based software tends to be a bit more secure than a desktop software since it does not store your information on your computer hard drive. With the desktop software, if the computer were to become infected with a virus or the like, then the personal data you have entered does have a risk of becoming public. Plus, it also increases the chances of hackers getting a hold of information that can destroy your credit or even result in losing your identity.

Most people find that the web based software is easier to use since the company that has this software is responsible for any problems that may occur. There is no downloading the software which is safer for those who have a fear of hackers. Plus, if you are someone that travels, you always have access whether you have your computer with you or not.

Whatever you choose, it is completely up to you. What works for a friend may not work for you, and vice versa. You will want to check out your options, try a test if this is available and then make a decision.

Diversifying Forex Trading Strategies

When it comes to trading on the forex market, the difference between those who make money at this and those who lose money at this is if the person knows how to manage their money. The odds of making money at the forex market is about 60% of all those who invest into the market. This is a pretty high percentage given that most markets cannot offer such a high success rate. However, of this percentage only 5% of those traders will be what most people consider very successful with the market. The other 95% of people will lose money. The main reason for money lost in this market is not having the proper skills to manage their money effectively.

Within the forex market there are several aspects that you are going to need to know in order to manage your money effectively. When you hear the term 'money management' this is referring to the money amount that you are trading with and the risks that you are accepting for the trade you are going with. There is a small difference between managing your money and making trading decisions, and a fine line that traders need to understand. There are numerous strategies on the market that are meant to help a person find the balance they need in order to reduce high risk trades, while managing their money in an effective way.

The term 'core equity' is one of those terms that the person will need to know about in order to succeed with the forex market. The core equity is the starting balance of the account and just what amounts are considered to be in the open position. This equity is going to have a profound impact on how you can manage your money. An example of this is if you start with an account that has $6,000 in it, yet you make a trade for $2,000, then your core equity is $4,000.

For those who are just beginning, it is going to be better if they do numerous trades that will diversify their currencies between several countries. Through only trading one currency you are going to have only a few signals of entry. An example of this is if yo have an account balance of $100,000, and your open position is at $10,000. This makes your core equity at $90,000. The second position you enter is going to be calculated with 1% of your core equity, meaning that the second trade you make cannot be more than $900. If you enter into a third position, the equity would drop to $80,000, meaning that the trade could not be more than $800. In order to avoid this type of situation, a person needs to diversify their currencies that are considered be different from one another. An example of this is:

If you trade EUR/USD and GPB/USD, at the amount of $10,000 with a 1% risk, then you could safely trade $5,000 in EUR/USD and $5,000 in GBP/USD. Through making this decision you are lowering your risk to 0.5% on each trade.

When looking at diversifying your trading strategies on the forex market, two strategies come to mind that everyone needs to understand. These are the Martingale and the Anti-Martingale. The Martingale refers to taking more risks when you are on the losing end of the market. Many gamblers are firm believers of this strategy. It is much easier to understand this strategy with a gambling example. With this strategy if a player were to lose $40, next time around they would bet $20. If the player were to lose a bet of $80, they would bet $160. They basically double what they have lost each time in order to see if they can come out ahead. By increasing the bet so much, the strategy states that a person could essentially make everything back in the long run. However, the odds are still 50/50 in terms of whether you can lose or win. Those who take this strategy often do not think about the actual chances of it working, and yet it is one of the most common mistakes that a new trader can make in the market.

When it comes to the forex market and applying these strategies, a trade that started with a balance of $10,00 and lost 4 trades that equaled to $4,000, leaving their balance at $6,000, would mean that the next trade would be the way in which the trader recovered their losses. However, even if the person were able to do this, they are still going to be down by around $2,000. When the stakes are this high, it is almost impossible to come back from this much of a loss. A trader who has experience, would never condone this sort of trading.

We Want Your Feedback on This Book!

Our main purpose is to make sure that our readers get value from the books we publish and that they have a good experience with all of our products. We are always working to improve our books and other products with every revision and update.

Every piece of feedback makes a difference in this process. And we would appreciate yours as well - whether it is good or bad.

Please take one minute to let us know what you thought by following this link:

http://checkmatemg.com/feedbackforex/

www.ingramcontent.com/pod-product-compliance
Lightning Source LLC
Chambersburg PA
CBHW071632170526
45166CB00003B/1298